D0986883

THE FIRST
BLUE JEANS

By
RICKI DRU

Illustrated by
Donna Moody

cpi
contemporary perspectives, inc.

This book is distributed by Silver Burdett Company, Morristown, New
Jersey, 07960.

Library of Congress Number: 78-14398

Art and Photo Credits

Cover illustration, Donna Moody
Photos on pages 12, 14, and 18, Photoworld
Photos on pages 23, 34, 36, 40, and 47, courtesy of Levi Strauss and
Co.
Every effort has been made to trace the ownership of all copyrighted
material in this book and to obtain permission for its use.

Library of Congress Cataloging in Publication Data

Dru, Ricki
The first blue jeans.

SUMMARY: Relates events that led to the production and popular-
ity of Levi Strauss's denim jeans.
1. Levi Strauss and Company — Juvenile literature. 2. Jeans (Clothing) — History — Juvenile literature. [1. Jeans (Clothing) — History. 2. Levi Strauss and Company] I. Title.
HD9940.U6L455   338.7'68'71   78-14398
ISBN 0-89547-059-4

Manufactured in the United States of America
ISBN 0-89547-059-4

CONTENTS

BLUE PANTS FOR THE GOLD BUG

The night sky was bright with stars. In the distance were the dark shapes of the great Sierra Nevada. On the ground were the bodies of sleeping men. The lamps had died out long ago. The night air was hot, so most of the men were asleep outside their tents. The sounds of snoring and grinding teeth were everywhere. This was the city of San Francisco at two o'clock one July morning. The year was 1850.

Only a year before, gold had been found at Sutter's Mill in California. News of it had traveled quickly all through America. Thousands of people had come west, "bitten by the gold bug." By day people worked and sweated, looking for the gold that would make them rich. At night these people walked slowly back to the city. They were tired, dirty, wet — and disappointed. Sleeping where they could, the miners dreamt of making the "big strike" that would make their fortunes.

On this July night only one lamp was still lit. Its flame glowed through the walls of a tent standing in a dark street. Inside were two men. One of them sat at a small table, busy with a needle and thread. Beside him stood a slim young man with dark hair and whiskers. He watched the older man push the needle through the stiff, heavy cloth heaped on the table.

It was hard, slow work. But on into the night the old man sewed — watched and helped by the 20-year-old man named Levi Strauss.

There was much to do. By daybreak the heap of canvas would have to be a pair of pants. Levi had promised one of the miners that the pants would be ready by then.

But Levi Strauss was excited for another reason. These were not ordinary pants. They were special — made just for the men who had come west. The men needed pants strong enough to last through the many hours they worked in the gold fields. Well, Levi thought, these pants were so strong they might never wear out!

In time "Levi Strauss" would become one of the most famous of all American names. It would be known all over the world. But on that hot night in 1850 only a few people had ever heard of it. Levi was just a young man from Germany who sat and sewed on into the night.

CHAPTER 1

STARTING
OUT

Levi Strauss was born in 1830 in Bavaria, a state in Germany. His family was poor and times were hard. All through Europe people began to save money so they could move to America. They were told that in America there was a chance to work and live better, maybe own a farm or start a business.

Families were leaving for America, hoping to find a golden chance for a new life. That's how Levi Strauss came over to America. His two older brothers, Jonas and Louis, came first. They sent for Levi when he was just 14 years old.

It was hard leaving home and knowing he might never return. Still Levi felt he was lucky. He had two brothers waiting for him in America. There he would become rich and live in a wonderful house — just like his brothers.

As he kissed his mother good-bye at the dock, Levi made believe he didn't see her crying. He understood why she was so upset. She was afraid she might never see her son again. Levi's father also had come to see the boy off on his journey. The old man was very sick, though.

Levi took his sister to one side. He kissed her cheek and whispered, "Please, take care of papa!"

Then without looking back, he ran up the gangplank to the waiting ship.

The man at the top of the gangplank was dressed in white. Standing on the deck, he helped people find their way around the ship. The man smiled and tipped his white hat to the well-dressed men and women as they stepped aboard. But when Levi came toward him, the man in white did not smile. He looked at the ticket pinned to Levi's coat. Then he pointed to a line of people.

"Over there," the man said. Suddenly Levi was more afraid of this man's cold stare than he was of leaving home.

The line of people moved down the steep stairs very slowly. They all carried heavy bags and boxes. There

were many small children to be helped step by step down into the ship. Levi wished he had stayed up on deck for just a moment longer.

Levi moved down the stairs. Then there was another set of stairs and still another. Levi became frightened. He knew no one on this ship. He didn't even know how long the trip might take!

Just then Levi heard the ship's whistle blow three times. He felt the ship shake as its engines began to turn. The ship was moving! Frightened or not, Levi Strauss was on his way to America all alone.

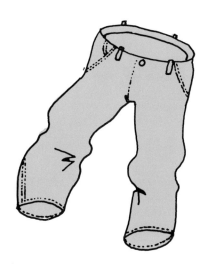

CHAPTER 2

AMERICA!

Levi soon learned why the man in the white suit had stared at him so coldly. Like many others on their way to America, Levi had one of the cheapest tickets. It was marked "steerage." That meant he was to stay down in a special part of the ship along with the poorest passengers.

People said steerage got you across the ocean just as quickly as the expensive cabins near the top deck. But it didn't feel that way if you were down in the crowded, uncomfortable steerage cabins. The *thump, thump* of the ship's engines never stopped. There was always the strong smell of the coal fires which ran the

Hoping to find a better life, many people crowded on to ships going to America.

engines. They kept the steerage cabins so hot that people could hardly breathe. People were packed tightly together, with no way to wash. What little food there was often spoiled or was filled with bugs.

Every day of the trip seemed worse than the day before. Many passengers became sick. It was not long before people were being buried at sea, dead before the voyage was over. Somehow, others survived.

Doctors examined the immigrants right after they arrived in New York.

It took a month for Levi's ship to land in New York. The people had finally made it to America! Levi looked around for his brothers. Americans were crowding around. They looked so rich and healthy. His brothers couldn't be among them! But those men in new suits and clean shirts — could they be Jonas and Louis? All at once the three brothers recognized one another. In a moment they were hugging, kissing, laughing, and crying all at the same time.

"Come and meet my wife Rebecca," said Jonas.

He proudly introduced Levi to a plump, rosy-faced little woman. She turned to her husband. "Jonas, my dear, let's take him right home and get him something to eat!"

His brothers and Rebecca led Levi through the busy, crowded streets. Around him people chatted and shouted in many different languages. Everyone was in such a hurry! He was glad when his family walked into a brown brick building, and the noise of the streets died away.

They climbed up five long flights of stairs. Finally they came to the two-room apartment shared by the Strauss family. The whole family lived in these two rooms. But it didn't seem crowded to Levi. In Bavaria many families shared only a single room. Grandparents, aunts, and uncles often shared that room too.

In America, though, Jonas and Rebecca slept in the small bedroom. In two corners of the larger room were curtains which hid the beds of Louis and Levi. Water for washing and drinking had to be carried up the stairs. When someone wanted a bath, he or she had to save 50¢ — almost a day's pay — to go use the public bathhouse many blocks away.

The food Rebecca served Levi was strange, but it tasted wonderful to the hungry boy. While they were eating dinner, Jonas and Louis asked about their family back in Bavaria. Levi's news was not good. "Times are hard," he told them.

Jonas and Louis exchanged serious looks. They had saved and saved, hoping to have enough money to bring the whole family to America. But there was not enough.

In spite of the news, the three brothers and Rebecca were very happy to be together that evening. They laughed, talked, and sang well into the night. When Levi finally settled into his bed that night, he was happy with his new home. "It *is* better in America!" he thought.

Levi's brothers ran a dry goods store. At first Levi helped them unload carts and wrap packages. But soon he learned enough English to make his way in the

The family spent a happy evening together. ▶

After Levi landed in New York City, he lived in a busy, crowded neighbor-
hood like this one.

different parts of New York. The young boy was sent to deliver cloth, pins, ribbons, and lace to customers all over the city.

As often happens with little brothers, Levi soon knew more about the city than Jonas or Louis. He also spoke better English. On his travels he met many people. These people saw how hard he worked, how helpful and honest he was. Soon they brought their business to the Strauss's store. Levi was proud of what he was doing. He was working hard and helping the family.

Three years passed. Then one evening at dinner, Jonas announced that he and Louis had thought of a way for the family to make more money. "But," he said, "the only way we can do it is with Levi's help!"

"We get many orders from outside the city," Jonas explained. "But we have no way to get our goods to the customers."

"People on farms and in small villages want the cloth we sell," said Louis. "They need hardware and clothes too. All we have to do is take our goods to them as peddlers — the way the Strauss family has always done it."

"But our peddler has to be young and healthy," Jonas said. "He must not be married. He must speak good English. And he must be friendly. People must like him."

"Well," said Louis, "there's only one of us who can do all that!"

Levi suddenly realized they meant him! Levi said he could hardly wait to begin. In a few days Levi was on his way, his wagon filled with goods from the store. Traveling beside the Hudson River, Levi made good time even though the country roads were rough and difficult.

For the next few weeks Levi did the same thing every day. He would set out at dawn, stopping at every village and farm along the way. He would show the people what he had in his wagon, comparing different items and explaining how to use them. Then he would talk with the people to find out what they needed. That's how he learned what to bring on his next trip.

Levi traveled up into the mountains, bringing the people cloth, hardware, and tools. His life was hard, but he liked the country people. They were quiet and honest, like the people back in Bavaria. And he loved the wild beauty of the countryside. It too reminded him of home. All around him were wooded mountains, sparkling streams, and peaceful valleys.

After several trips Levi heard the farmers talk about a wonderful new place. Kentucky was its name. Many people had already gone there looking for what they called "elbow room." Life was easier in Kentucky, they told him. It was a place to make your fortune. Soon people all along Levi's route began to move to Kentucky. So Levi went to his brothers. He suggested that he make a trip there too. "A peddler must follow the people who buy from him," he told Jonas. "People in Kentucky will need our goods."

Levi was soon on his way to Kentucky. It was a long trip. His wagon bumped and bounded its way over steep hills. The trails led through deep, dark woods filled with the sounds of strange birds and animals.

In this wilderness Levi learned to enjoy being alone. He loved the natural beauty of this land even more than he had back in New York. He also learned to admire the pioneer spirit of the men and women in Kentucky. Soon Levi began to think of *this* country, not Bavaria, as his home.

One day in 1849 a letter came to Levi from his brothers. Thousands of people were rushing to California. Gold had been discovered at a place called Sutter's Mill. Jonas and Louis wanted Levi to go there to sell cloth and hardware. Levi did not need to stop and think about the idea. He was ready to go West!

Levi Strauss as he looked when he arrived in California during the Gold Rush.

CHAPTER 3

CALIFORNIA!

Levi Strauss stood on the deck of the clipper ship *Nantucket*. He had returned to New York to pick up goods from his brothers' store. Now he took one last look at New York harbor. The breeze ruffled the long sideburns he had just grown. Levi knew he was lucky to be aboard a fine ship like the *Nantucket*. She was a strong, well-built ship. The cabins were comfortable and there was plenty of food. This time there would be no bugs in Levi's food!

Levi started to laugh to himself. "Just six years ago," he thought, "I was crowded into steerage with the poorest immigrants. Now I have a fine cabin all to myself on a great ship bound for California. And I'm not a boy anymore — I'm a businessman."

Levi sold his goods to the crew and passengers on the *Nantucket*.

In the ship's hold were crates marked with the name of the Strauss brothers' store. They were loaded with goods — bundles of clothing, bolts of cloth, boots, and hardware. There was everything he needed to start his new business out West. Dreams of the future filled Levi's head as he walked down to his cabin.

A few days later Levi was walking along the deck. Sitting between the ship's masts was a man at work with a hammer and saw. Levi told him he was surprised to see a carpenter at work out in the middle of the ocean.

The man laughed loudly. "I'm Yates, the ship's carpenter. But I won't be working long if I don't get some nails. We've run out of them already."

When Levi heard this he offered the carpenter all the nails he wanted. After all, there were many barrels of nails in Levi's cargo. Delighted, Yates bought a whole barrel. Then he told everyone what a thoughtful friend Levi was. When the other passengers learned about his cargo, they were delighted too. They knew they would need many things for California. So they began buying them from Levi.

Levi sold so many items during the voyage that soon he had only canvas and hardware left. Between his lively business and the new friends he made, Levi found that time seemed to pass quickly. It was not long before Levi stood on the deck of the *Nantucket*, watching San Francisco Bay coming closer and closer. Levi could feel the excitement of the Gold Rush! Everyone on the boats and docks moved quickly.

When the *Nantucket* had docked, the gangplank was lowered and Levi disembarked along with the other passengers. Levi knew that he would soon be busy meeting people and selling goods. People liked his warm, polite manner. His honest behavior made them want to do business with him. He would do well, he knew.

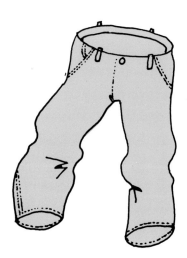

CHAPTER 4

WAIST-HIGH OVERALLS

It was only a few nights later that Levi stood in that hot, stuffy tent working on into the night. As they worked, he and the old man glanced at the drawing of a pair of pants tacked to the wall. "Do the welted seams have to go all the way up the leg?" Levi asked the older man.

"Yup," grunted the older man, who was a tailor. "But you're going to break all my needles with these canvas pants of yours."

"Don't worry, Sam," Levi told him. "My brothers will send us more from New York."

A loud bang from outside made them jump. Levi looked out of the window.

"A gun battle!" Levi cried. He was excited by the thought of the gunfight.

"Never you mind," the tailor told him. "They're all crazy out there. Those miners have got 'gold fever.' Just remember, we've got to get these pants ready for tomorrow morning — old Pete's leaving for his diggings then."

Levi returned to his work. But his thoughts were still outdoors in the boomtown of San Francisco. He had arrived only a week ago, bringing canvas and hardware to sell to the "forty-niners." Since then not a moment went by that didn't amaze and surprise him.

To begin with, the city of San Francisco was not like New York at all. It was little more than a collection of tents. When gold was discovered at Sutter's Mill near San Francisco, people came from all over the world. They wanted to share in the wealth that the miners dug up. When Levi arrived there were already 10,000 forty-niners living in the local mining camps. These places had names like Poker Flat, Git-Up-and-Git, Red Dog, and Grub Gulch.

Almost everyone who came to San Francisco had gold fever. They didn't even bother with tents. They just slept on the ground.

Young Levi put his goods on a wagon and went straight to the Grand Hotel. It was one of the few real wooden structures in town. On the way he saw that the streets were only dirt paths. When miners rode by on their mules, dust rose up and blew into everyone's eyes. In one spot a huge mud puddle stretched all the way across the street.

Everywhere he went Levi noticed men and women selling provisions. The prices he saw were a hundred times the prices back in New York! Eggs were five dollars apiece, and a shirt or a pair of pants might cost $40. The equipment, clothing, and food had come from far away. But some greedy people were charging much more than the transportation had cost. The miners had to pay the prices anyway, though. They could not buy things anywhere else.

Levi watched a young woman selling shovels. "Step right up, friend," she said to a young prospector in a red flannel shirt. The prospector emptied a little pouch of glittering gold nuggets into his palm and counted out a few to be weighed.

"There's plenty more where these came from!" he claimed proudly. "I need a really good shovel to dig 'em all out!"

Levi knew he would have no trouble selling goods — and for real gold too! He could hardly wait to write to Jonas and Louis about San Francisco.

The next day Levi went out into the dusty streets to look for customers. Many of the miners bought his hardware — nails, rivets, grommets. But none of them bought any of the canvas. Why? he wondered. He asked an old prospector who had bought the last half-dozen nails.

"Don't need canvas," the prospector said. "Just look at the tents all around you. There it is — canvas, miles of it. Stuff won't wear out in a man's lifetime."

The old miner thought a minute. Then he said, "What you should-a brought was pants. Pants don't wear worth a hoot up in the diggin's. You can't get a pair strong enough to last no time at all."

Levi looked around. It was true. Many miners were wearing old, ragged pants. "I know," he thought, "I'll send home for some heavy workpants to sell!"

He soon realized that it would be three months before his letter reached New York and three months before the pants got to San Francisco. Then Levi had an even better idea. He would make pants right there in San Francisco. And he'd use his canvas!

Levi saw a prospector paying for a shovel with real gold nuggets.

Levi's pants have changed little in style since the gold miners wore them in the 1880s.

Levi didn't waste any time. He set out to find a tailor. Levi could sew, but he really didn't know how to make the kind of pants the miners would need. Discouraged, Levi walked through the dusty streets. Then as he turned a corner he saw a tailor! A little, wrinkled old man sat cross-legged on the floor of his tent, sewing. Over his head a sign read, "Sam Wiggins, Esq., Gentlemen's Tailor."

Laughing with delight, Levi introduced himself to the old man and told him what he needed. Soon they had drawn up a design for a pair of canvas pants. It did not take long to find an old miner named Pete who said he would buy the pants as soon as they were finished.

Levi and Sam worked all night to have them ready for Pete. The miner wanted to show off his new pants before wearing them.

Three weeks later Levi was hard at work making "waist-high overalls" out of canvas. Old Pete had come back from his diggings. "I may not have found gold," he told everyone, "but I sure found the best pair of pants I ever wore!"

Soon other miners wanted Levi's pants too. In fact the pants were so popular that Levi had to find another tailor to keep up with the orders that were coming in.

In a few months Levi stood in the new shop he had just opened. He had never felt so proud. He had done

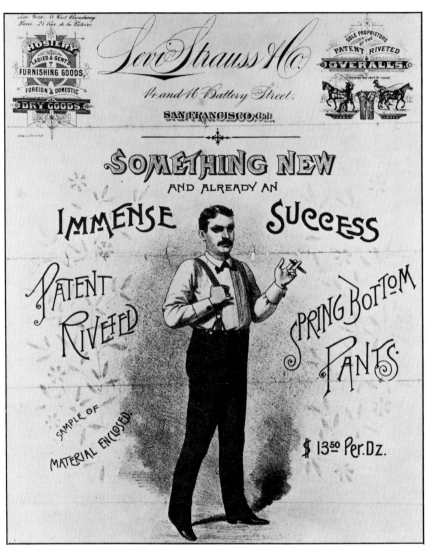

One of the first posters for Levi's "waist-high overalls."

it at last — he had started his new business. Levi
didn't know it yet, but he was founding a business that
would make his name famous and change the way
people dressed as well. Soon people all over the world
would be asking for Levi's pants.

CHAPTER 5

THE REAL BLUE JEANS

"Tarnation!" bellowed Abel, a white-bearded prospector. He was standing on a rock in the middle of a creek. He glared down at his torn pants.

"Just look at that, Carrots!" Abel said to his burro. "Ripped up to the knee. Well, they'll have to last till next month when I go into town for supplies!"

"What's all the commotion about? Just 'cause you tore your britches?" It was old Pete, coming around a boulder.

"Folks that makes pants just don't understand us miners," Abel grumbled.

"Some of 'em do. Looky my pants — had 'em for six months and not a dent in 'em. Fella back in San Francisco made 'em for 22¢," said Pete.

"Oh yeah? What's his name?" asked Abel.

"Levi Strauss. Just ask anybody there where to buy Levi's pants. He said he was gonna set up a store and sell a pair to every man in California!"

That's how word spread about Levi's "waist-high overalls" (which is what Levi liked to call them). The miners didn't like long words, so they usually just called them "Levi's pants."

The miners traveled all over the West searching for gold and silver. They rushed off as soon as any signs of gold or silver were found. Gamblers, bartenders, and dance-hall girls followed the miners to their camps. After them came merchants, then lawyers and newspaper editors. Soon farmers came, drawn by the high prices the miners paid for food.

So it was miners too, and not just frontiersmen and cowboys, who opened up the West. Everywhere the miners went they took Levi's pants with them. Soon farmers were wearing them, and so were the cowboys who worked the big cattle ranches of the West. When the transcontinental railroad was being built, from

Levi Strauss became known as the "cowboy's tailor" when his pants became popular on the range.

1863 to 1869, the railroad workers depended on their Levi's pants to protect them in rough country.

Even after the railroads were finished Levi's pants were handy. Once the couplings holding two railroad cars gave way as a train sped across the country. The engineer didn't dare stop the train, for fear the angry Sioux Indians might attack. The engineer had once been a cowboy, and he remembered how strong his Levi's pants were. He grabbed a spare pair, tied one leg to one of the cars and the other leg to the other car. That train made it all the way to the next station, held together by a pair of Levi's pants!

Over the years Levi made some changes in his pants. Canvas was very stiff and heavy. It was hard to sew and not very comfortable to wear. Levi had learned a lot about fabrics. He decided that the best fabric for his pants was denim — it was strong, cheap, and softer than canvas.

When the first shipment of denim arrived at Levi's shop, however, he realized that the color was wrong for miners' pants. White cloth wouldn't stay white for a minute on the knees of a miner in Sutter's Creek. He would dye the cloth. But what color?

Black and brown were popular colors, but black and brown dyes were expensive. And they were hard to work with too. Then Levi remembered the beautiful deep blue color of the clothes worn by the Chinese people of San Francisco. He went to ask about the blue clothes. That's how Levi learned about indigo blue dye.

Indigo is an inexpensive dye made in India from a bush. Indigo, in fact, is the oldest dye known in history. It always produces a beautiful, deep blue color.

So Levi dyed his denim indigo blue. Then he made up the first batch of "blue jeans." They were far simpler than today's jeans, of course. They had no

pockets or belt loops, only buttons for attaching suspenders. And there was something else missing too.

In the late 1860s, Levi heard from a tailor from Carson City, Nevada. His name was Jacob W. Davis, and he said he admired the strong pants Levi had invented. But he had a very special idea.

One night in Carson City, Jacob was roused out of bed by a commotion outside his window. It was Alkali Ike, off on a spree. Jacob called down, asking him what was the matter. Ike hollered that he had just come from his diggings with his pockets full of gold nuggets. But the pockets had torn. Jacob's repair work had not held up — all the gold was lost.

Jacob wasn't a fool. Ike's pockets probably had torn because Ike stuffed too many heavy mining tools into them. Jacob Davis decided to play a little trick on Alkali Ike.

"Leave your torn pants downstairs," he called to Ike. "I'll fix 'em tomorrow, for free."

Next day Jacob mended the pockets and took the pants to a harness maker. There he had the corners of the pockets set with the copper rivets used to strengthen leather harnesses. He gave Ike the pants.

A few weeks later Ike came back to Jacob. He praised him for the bright idea of riveting the pockets. The pants had never ripped again, he said. Ever since then Jacob had been repairing miners' pants with copper rivets. Why not, he asked Levi, put the rivets in the pants before they're worn — right in Levi Strauss's factory?

In 1873 he and Jacob Davis took out a patent on the riveted pockets. Today Levi's still are copper-riveted. But during the 1930s the rivets on the back pockets were covered with fabric. Teachers complained that Levi's scratched school furniture, and cowboys said the rivets scratched the leather of their saddles. Soon the back-pocket rivets were left off altogether.

In 1886 Levi added the leather label on the back of his jeans. It was stamped with a picture of two horses trying to pull apart a pair of Levi's pants. The label showed how proud Levi was of the pants' strength.

When he grew older Levi looked back on his life with a special kind of pride. Things had gone well for the man who had started life in America as an immigrant from Bavaria. He had become the successful businessman he always dreamed of being. And he had four nephews — young men who would carry on that business. But Levi had never forgotten the crowded steerage cabins or the life he had shared with other immigrants.

A pair of Levi's pants could be purchased from a street vendor.

In fact, some people say that is why Levi Strauss kept the family store in San Francisco even after his pants had made him a wealthy and famous man. The store reminded him, they say, of the success he had gained and of how he had gotten it. But most of all, it reminded him of how the name of that frightened boy of 14 had come to stand for a whole American way of life.

Levi's pants had helped open and build the West. And over the years they had become something that stood for how Americans lived and worked. It would not be long before everyone would be wearing Levi's pants. Like the miners of San Francisco, kids and presidents, people from America and from hundreds of other places would always ask for Levi's pants. Perhaps it was because they could see in each pair the story of Levi Strauss and the first blue jeans.

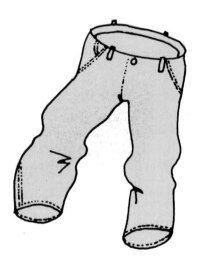